## Intermediate

# CONTENTS

## Experienced

# MESH-merizing

## You'll Need

### YARN 2
- *Baby Sheen* by Red Heart/
  Coats & Clark, 14oz/397g,
  1228yd/1123m (21oz/595g,
  1842yd/1684m acrylic in #001
  white

### HOOKS
- Size E/4 (3.5mm) crochet hook
  *or size to obtain gauge*

## SIZES
Sized for Small/Large (XX-Large/XXX-Large). Shown in size
Small/Large.

## FINISHED MEASUREMENTS
**Bust** 43 (59)"/109 (150)cm
**Length** 23½ (26½)"/59.5 (67)cm
**Upper arm** 13½ (21½)"/34 (55)cm

## GAUGE
12 mesh sps and 10 rows to 4"/10cm over wave pat st using
size E/4 (3.5mm) crochet hook.
*Take time to check gauge.*

## STITCH GLOSSARY
**dtr** [yo] 4 times, insert hook into st and pull up a lp, [yo and
pull through 2 lps] 5 times.
**Wave pattern stitch**
(Ch a multiple of 48 plus 36)
**Note** One sp is formed by a sl st, sc, dc,
tr or dtr plus ch 1.
**Row 1 (RS)** Sl st in 2nd ch from hook,
+*[Ch 1, sk 1 ch, sl st in next ch] 5
times, [ch 1, skip 1 ch, sc in next ch]
twice, [ch 1, skip 1 ch, dc in next ch]
twice, [ch 1, skip 1 ch, tr in next ch]
twice, [ch 1, skip 1 ch, dtr in next ch] 6
times +, [ch 1, skip 1 ch, tr in next ch]
twice, [ch 1, skip 1 ch, dc in next ch]
twice, [ch 1, skip 1 ch, sc in next ch]
twice, ch 1 , skip 1 ch, sl st in next ch;
rep from *, then end by rep between

+'s once. Ch 1, turn.
**Row 2** Sl st in first dtr, +* [ch 1, sl st in next dtr] 5 times, [ch
1, sc in next tr] twice, [ch 1, dc in next dc] twice, [ch 1, tr in
next sc] twice, [ch 1, dtr in next sl st] 6 times+, [ch 1, tr in next
sc] twice, [ch 1, dc in next dc] twice, [ch 1, sc in next tr] twice,
ch 1, sl st in next dtr; rep from *, then end by rep between +'s
once. Ch 1, turn. **Note** From this point on, all sl sts, sc, dc, tr
and dtr will be called sts.
**Row 3** Sc in first st, *+ ch 1, sc in next st, [ch 1, dc in next st]
twice, [ch 1, tr in next st] twice, [ch 1, dtr in next st] 6 times,
[ch 1, tr in next st] twice, [ch 1, dc in next st] twice, [ch 1, sc
in next st] twice+, [ch 1, sl st in next st] 6 times, ch 1, sc in
next st; rep from * end by rep between +'s once, ch 3 (does not
count as 1 tr), turn.
**Row 4** Tr in first st, *+ ch 1 tr in next st, [ch 1, dc in next st]
twice, [ch 1, sc in next st] twice, [ch 1, sl st in next st] 6 times,
[ch 1, sc in next st] twice, [ch 1, dc in next st] twice, [ch 1, tr in
next st] twice+, [ch 1, dtr in next st]  6 times, ch 1, tr in next st;
rep from *, end by rep between +'s once. Ch 1, turn. Rep rows
1-4 for wave pat st. (Also see chart.)

## BACK
Ch 132 (180) for 65 (89) sps. Work in wave pat st for a total of
58 (66) rows, ending with row 2 of wave pat st. Piece measures
approx 23½ (26½)"/59.5 (67)cm from beg. Fasten off.

## FRONT
Work as for back for a total of 54 (62) rows. Piece measures
approx 21½ (25)"/54.5 (63.5)cm from beg, end with row 2 of
wave pat st. Ch 1, turn.

**Neck shaping**
**Left shoulder**
**Next (row 3)** Working in pat, work 2 sc, 2 dc, 2 tr, 6 dtr, 2 tr,

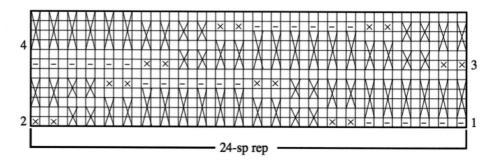

24-sp rep

### Stitch Key

☐ ch-1 sp  ⊠ sc  ⊠ dc  ⋈ tr  ⧲ dtr
⊟ sl st

Dan Howell

2 dc, 2 sc, 1 (6) sl st, 0 (2) sc, 0 (2) dc, 0 (2) tr, 0 (1) dtr for a total of 19 (31) sts. Ch 3 (1), turn.

**Next (row 4)** Working in pat, work 0 (1) sl st, 0 (2) sc, 0 (2) dc, 0 (2) tr, 1 (6) dtr, 2 tr, 2 dc, 2 sc, 6 sl st, 2 sc, 2 dc, 2 tr. Ch 1, turn.

**Next (row 1)** Work 6 sl st, 2 sc, 2 dc, 2 tr, 6 dtr, 0 (2) tr, 0 (2) dc, 0 (2) sc, 0 (6) sl st. Ch 1 turn.

**Next (row 2)** Work 6 sl st. Fasten off.

**Right shoulder**

Rejoin yarn to work last 19 (31) sts and work as for left shoulder in reverse.

## SLEEVES

Beg at top edge of sleeve, ch 84 (132) for 41 (65) sps. Work in wave pat st for 8 (4) rows.

**Dec row** Ch 2, skip first st and sp and work into next st (dec 1 sp), work pat row 1 to last sp, leave last sp unworked. Cont to dec 1 sp each side every 4th row 8 (9) times more—23 (45) sps. Work even for 2 (0) rows.

**Next row** Sc in each st and each sp dec 0 (10) sts evenly—47 (81) sts. Ch 1, turn. Work 1 sc in each sc. Fasten off.

## FINISHING

Block piece to measurements. Sew shoulder seams for 6½ (10½)"/16.5 (26.5)cm. Place markers at 6¾ (10¾)"/17 (27.5)cm down from shoulders. Sew sleeves to armholes between markers. Sew sleeve seams. Leaving 4"/10cm open at lower edge, sew side seams. Work 1 rnd of sc around neck edge. Ch 1. Work 1 rnd of sc in back lp of each sc around. Work lower edge trim and side slit trim in same way.

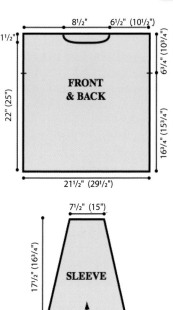

# CROCHET carry-all

## You'll Need

### YARN ❷
- *Baby Sheen* by Red Heart/Coats & Clark, 3½oz/100g, 307yd/281m acrylic
- 1 ball each in #570 lilac (A-1), #700 pink (A-2) and #620 pistachio (B)
- 2 balls in #001 white (C)

### HOOKS
- Size B/1 (2mm) crochet hook *or size to obtain gauge*

### OTHER MATERIALS
- Plastic handles
- ¼yd/.25m of ½"/13m wide ribbon

## FINISHED MEASUREMENTS
Bag measures 9¾"/25cm square.

## GAUGE
One flower motif is 3¼"/8.25cm square.
*Take time to check gauge.*

## MOTIF
Make 9 motifs using A-1 and 9 motifs using A-2. With A, ch 8, join with a sl st to first ch to form ring.

**Rnd 1** With A, ch 6, *1 dc in ring, ch 3; rep from * 4 times more, join with a sl st to 3rd ch of ch-6 (6 sps).

**Rnd 2** With A, in each ch-3 sp work 1 sc, 1 hdc, 3 dc, 1 hdc and 1 sc (6 petals).

**Rnd 3** With A, ch 7, *1 hdc inserting hook from back to front to back around post of first dc on row 1 for 1 back hdc, ch 5; rep from * 5 times more, end sl st in 2nd ch of ch-7 (7 ch lps).

**Rnd 4** With A, in each ch-5 sp work 1 sc, 1 hdc, 5 dc, 1 hdc and 1 sc; end rnd with sl st to first sc.

**Rnd 5** With A, ch 9, *1 back hdc in corresponding hdc on rnd 3, ch 7; rep from * 6 times more, end draw B through 2nd ch of ch-9. Cut A.

**Rnd 6** With B, ch 1, *work 1 sc, 1 hdc, 7 dc, 1 hdc and 1 sc in first lp, ch 4, sc in next ch-7 lp, ch 4; rep from *, end by sl st with C in first sc. Cut B.

**Rnd 7** With C, ch 1, sc in sc with joining, *[ch 4, 1 sc in 3rd ch from hook for picot] twice, ch 1, 1 sc in center of corner petal, [ch 4, 1 picot] twice, ch 1, sc through ch-4 loop in B and A loop underneath, [ch 4, 1 picot] twice, ch 1, 1 sc through ch-4 loop in B and A loop underneath; rep from *, end sl st in first sc. Fasten off.

## Join squares
**Note** Join square alternating A-1 and A-2 squares as in photo. To join 2 squares with C, sc in corner of first square, ch 4, picot, ch 4, sc in opposite corner of second square; then working down the side, [ch 2, sc in first square side, ch 2, sc in opposite side of second square] twice, ch 1, sc in center of corner then ch 5 and sc into corner of 3rd square; join 2 sides of the first and 3rd squares tog as before. When joining 4th square, at the center point between the 4 squares, work ch 2, join with sl st to 3rd ch of ch 5, ch 2 and join to opposite square. Work 3 rows of 3 sets of alternating joined motifs each for front and back.

## Gussets
Work into the back piece along the side edge, with C, work as foll: work 1 back sc (as for back hdc) into corner, * ch 5, 1 back sc behind next sc, in color C; rep from * 10 times to corner (bottoms of bag), ch 6, work 1 back sc in next sc in color C; then rep from * cont around lower edge and side edge as before, turn. **Row 1 (WS)** Ch 2, work 5 hdc in ch-6 loop, *[5 hdc in ch-5 loop] 9 times, dc, ch 1 and dc in corner; rep from * around, turn.

**Row 2** Working into back loop only, ch 1, work 20 sc, 20 hdc, 16 dc, dc, ch 1 and dc in corner sp, 56 dc across lower edge of bag, dc, ch 1 and dc in corner sp, 16 dc, 20 hdc and 20 sc up other side, turn.

**Row 3** Ch 1, working into front loops only, work 20 sc, 20 hdc, then dc to corner, dc in corner ch-1 sp, work dc across lower edge of bag, then work other side of back to correspond. Fasten off. Work front piece in same way. Then sl st front and back pieces tog from WS through the outside lps only.

## Top facing
Work row 1 as for row 1 of gusset with back sc and ch-lps. **Row 2** Working into each ch-lp work * 5 hdc in first lp, 4 hdc in next lp; rep from * to end, turn. **Row 3** Ch 2, work 1 hdc in each hdc. Fasten off. Turn facing to WS and tack neatly in place. To attach handles, draw a 6"/15cm length of ribbon through the handle slits and sew to inside of gusset with ends hanging loose to inside.

Nick Norwood

# CAPE crusader

## You'll Need

**YARN**

- 5¼oz/150g, 410yd/375m of any sport weight cotton blend in white

**HOOK**

- Size D/3 (3.25mm) crochet hook *or size to obtain gauge*

**OTHER MATERIALS**

- One safety pin
- One ¼"/6mm pearl ball button

## FINISHED MEASUREMENTS

**Neck** 21"/53cm
**Length** 8"/20cm
**Lower edge** 44"/112cm

## GAUGE

24 sts and 28 rows to 4"/10cm over sc using size D/3 (3.25mm) crochet hook.
*Take time to check gauge.*

## CAPELET

Beg at neck edge, ch 133.
**Foundation row** Sc in 2nd ch from hook and in each ch across—132 sts. Ch 1, turn.
**Row 1(RS)** Sc in first 5 sts, *ch 4, sk next 2 sts, sc in next st; rep from * across, end sc in last 4 sts—41 ch-4 lps. Ch 1, turn.
**Rows 2-4** Sc in first 5 sts, *ch 4, sc in next ch-4 lp; rep from * across, end sc in last 5 sts. Ch 1, turn.
**Row 5** Sc in first 5 sts, *ch 5, sc in ch-4 lp; rep from * across, end sc in last 5 sts. Ch 1, turn.
**Rows 6-8** Sc in first 5 sts, *ch 5, sc in ch-5 lp; rep from * across, end sc in last 5 sts. Ch 1, turn.
**Row 9** Sc in first 5 sts, *ch 6, sc in ch-5 lp; rep from * across, end sc in last 5 sts. Ch 1, turn.
**Row 10 (WS)** Sc in first 5 sts, *ch 6, sc in ch-6 lp; rep from * across, end sc in last 5 sts.

### Joining

Taking care not to twist work, join piece with a sl st in first sc forming a circle. Ch 1, turn. Work now in the round.

**Rnd 11** Sc in first 5 sts, *ch 6, sc in ch-6 lp; rep from * around, end ch 6, do not work across last 5 sc.
**Rnds 12-14** Sc in first 10 sc (front placket), *ch 6, sc in ch-6 lp; rep from * around, end ch 6.
**Rnd 15** Sc in first st of front placket, ch 7, sk next 3 sts, sc in next st (mark this ch-7 lp just made with the safety pin to indicate beg of rnd), ch 7, sk next 4 sts, sc in next st, *ch 7, sc in ch-6 lp; rep from * around. Mark first lp made of each remaining rnd with the safety pin.
**Rnds 16-20** *Ch 7, sc in ch-7 lp; rep from * around.
**Rnd 21** *Ch 8, sc in ch-7 lp; rep from * around.
**Rnds 22-25** *Ch 8, sc in ch-8 lp; rep from * around. When rnd 25 is completed, join rnd with a sl st in first ch-8 lp of last rnd. Fasten off.

## FINISHING

### Neck Edging

From RS, join yarn with a sl st at base of right neck opening, ch 1.
**Row 1** Making sure that work lies flat, sc evenly along entire neck edge, working 3 sc in each corner. Ch 2, do not turn.
**Row 2** Working from left to right, sk first st, *sc in next st, ch 2, sk next st; rep from * across, end sc in last st. Fasten off.

## FLORETTE

**Foundation ring** Ch 6 leaving a long tail for sewing. Join ch with a sl st forming a ring.
**Rnd 1** Ch 3, *make popcorn: work 5 dc over ring. Remove hook from working lp, then insert hook under top 2 loops of first dc. Place working loop back onto hook. Yo, and draw through all lps on hook. Pull lead yarn to gather sts tog. Ch 3; rep from * around 5 times more. Join rnd with a sl st in 3rd ch of ch-3.
**Rnd 2** Ch 1, *sc in 3rd st of popcorn, ch 3, sc in ch-3 lp, ch 3; rep from * around 5 times more. Join rnd with a sl st in ch-1. Fasten off. Turn to WS of florette. Thread tail of foundation ring into tapestry needle. To close hole in center, run needle under base of dc sts. Pull tail to close opening. Fasten off securely on WS. Sew pearl button to center of florette. Sew florette to base of neck opening, as shown.

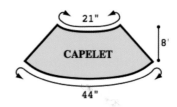

Marco Zambelli

# SHEER delight

## You'll Need

### YARN

- *Simply Soft* by Caron, 21oz/595g skeins, each approx 1155yd/1056m acrylic in #9709 light country blue

### HOOKS

- Sizes H/8 and J/10 (5 and 6mm) crochet hooks *or size to obtain gauge*

## SIZES

Sized for Small/Medium.

## FINISHED MEASUREMENTS

**Hem** 53"/134.5cm
**Bust** 35"/89cm
**Length** 49"/124.5cm

## GAUGE

14 dc and 8 pat rows to 4"/10cm over pat st using size J/10 (6mm) hook.
*Take time to check gauge.*

## STITCH GLOSSARY

### Pattern stitch

(Chain a multiple of 4 ch plus 2 extra)
**Row 1** Sc in 2nd ch from hook, *ch 7, skip 3 ch, 1 sc in next ch; rep from * to end. Ch 6, turn.
**Row 2** Sc in first ch-7 sp, *ch 3, sc in next ch 7 sp; rep from *, end ch 2, dc in last sc. Ch 6, turn.
**Row 3** *Sc in next sc, ch 7; rep from *, end sc in last sc, ch 3, dc in 3rd ch of t-ch. Ch 1, turn.
**Row 4** Sc in first dc, *ch 3, sc in next ch-7 sp; rep from *, end ch 3, sc in 3rd ch of t-ch. Ch 3, turn.

**Row 5** Skip first sc. *3 dc in ch-3 sp, dc in next sc; rep from * to end (t-ch 3 at beg counts as 1 dc). Ch 1, turn.
**Row 6** Sc in first dc, *ch 7, skip 3 dc, sc in next dc; rep from * end with sc in top of t-ch. Ch 6, turn. Rep rows 2-6 for pat st.

## BACK

With size J/10 (6mm) hook, ch 94. Work in pat st on 23 pats (there are 93 dc on pat row 5) until piece measures 7¼"/18.5cm from beg, end with pat row 4 of 3rd 5-row pat rep.
**Dec row 5** Skip first sc (ch-3 counts as 1 dc), 2 dc in first ch-3 sp, dc in next sc, 3 dc in next ch-3 sp, dc in next sc, 2 dc in next ch-3 sp, *dc in next sc, 3 dc in ch-3 sp; rep from * to last 3 ch-3 sps, dc in next sc, 2 dc in next ch-3 sp, dc in next sc, 3 dc in next ch-3 sp, dc in next sc, 2 dc in last ch-3 sp, dc in last sc—89 dc. (4 dc dec'd). Ch 1, turn. There are now 3 dc pat row bands (or pat row 5 has been worked 3 times). Rep dec row 5 on 5th, 6th, 7th, 8th, 10th, 11th, 12th and 13th pat row band (working other pat row 5 bands even in pat). There are 57 dc and 14 pats. Work 14th pat row 5 band even.
**Next (15th) pat band (inc row)** Dc in first sc (inc 1), 3 dc in first ch-3 sp, dc in next sc, 4 dc in next ch-3 sp, dc in next sc, work pat row 5 to last 2 ch-3 sps, 4 dc in next ch-3 sp, dc in next sc, 4 dc in next ch-3 sp, dc in top of t-ch. There are 61 dc and 15 pats. Work even through end of row 5 of 16th pat row band. Piece measures approx 42"/106.5cm from beg. Cut yarn.

### Armhole Shaping

**Next (pat row 6)** Skip first 6 dc, rejoin yarn in next dc and ch 1, sc in same dc with joining and rep from * of pat row 6 to last 6 dc, leave these dc unworked. There

are 49 dc and 12 pats. Ch 6, turn. **Next (pat row 2)** Skip first ch-7sp, *sc

in next ch-7sp, ch 3; rep from *, end sc in last ch-7 sp (do not ch 2 and dc in last sc). Ch 6, turn. **Next row** Work pat row 3 on 11 sps. **Next row** Work pat row 4 on 11 sps. **Next row** Rep dec row 5. There are 41 dc and 10 pats. Work even until there are a total of 18 pat row 5 bands. Then work rows 6 and 2 again. Fasten off.

## FRONT

Work as for back until there are a total of 17 pat row 5 bands. There are 41 dc and 10 pats.

### Neck Shaping

**Next (pat row 6)—First side** Sc in first dc, *[ch 7, skip 3 dc, sc in next dc] 3 times, leave rem dc unworked. Ch 6, turn. **Next (pat row 2)** Skip first ch-7 sp,

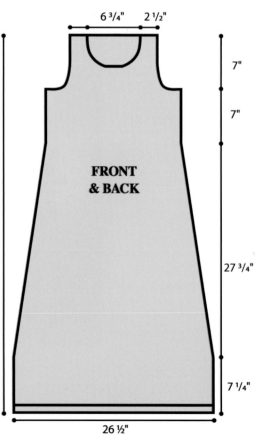

FRONT & BACK

6 ¾"   2 ½"

7"

7"

49"

27 ¾"

7 ¼"

26 ½"

sc in next ch 7 sp, ch 3, sc in next ch-7 sp, ch 2, dc in last sc. Work even on 9 dc and 2 pats until same number of rows as on back. Fasten off. To work 2nd side, skip center 15 dc, rejoin yarn and ch 1, sc in same dc with joining and complete to correspond to first side.

## FINISHING

Do not block. Lay pieces flat and mist lightly with water. Leave until dry. With larger hook, sl st tog shoulder and side seams from WS.

### Edging

With smaller hook, join in one side seam of hem.

**Rnd 1** Working through outer lps only, work 1 sc in back ch around. Join with sl st. **Rnd 2** *Ch 4, skip 1 sc, sl st in next sc; rep from * around. Join and fasten off. Work edge in same way around armhole and neck edges.

Paul Amato

# THINK tank

## You'll Need

**YARN**

- *Cotton-Ease* by Lion Brand Yarn Co.,
- 3½oz/100g, 207yd/191m cotton and acrylic blend
- 3 (4, 4, 5, 5) skeins in #148 turquoise (MC)
- 1 skein in #100 snow (CC)

**HOOKS**

- One each sizes C/2 and D/3 (2.5 and 3mm) crochet hooks *or sizes to obtain gauge*

## SIZES

Sized for X-Small (Small, Medium, Large, X-Large). Shown in size Small.

## FINISHED MEASUREMENTS

**Bust** 33 (35, 37, 39, 41)"/83.5 (88, 94, 99, 104)cm
**Length** 18 (18, 18½, 19, 19½)"/45.5 (45.5, 47, 48.5, 49.5)cm

## GAUGE

12 mesh sps and 10 mesh rows to 4"/10cm over mesh pat using size D/3 (3mm) hook.
*Take time to check gauge.*

## Note

One mesh sp worked each side will be worked as a selvage (to be turned under when seaming).

## BACK

With size D/3 (3mm) crochet hook and MC, ch 97 (103, 109, 115, 121).
**Row 1 (RS)** 1 dc in 5th ch from hook, *ch 1, skip 1 ch, 1 dc in next ch; rep from * to end—47 (50, 53, 56, 59) mesh sps, turn.
**Row 2** Ch 5, *1 dc in next dc, ch 1; rep from *, end 1 dc in top of t-ch, turn. Rep row 2 for mesh pat until piece measures approx 3"/7.5cm from beg. (There are 7 mesh rows). This marks end of side slit. **Next row** Ch 7, 1 dc in 5th ch from hook, 1 dc in first ch-1 sp (2 mesh inc), *ch 1, 1 dc in next dc; rep from * to last sp, end [ch 1, 1 dc in last ch-1 sp] twice

(2 mesh inc), ch 1, 1 dc in top of t-ch—51 (54, 57, 60, 63) mesh sps, turn. Work even in mesh pat until piece measures 10½"/26.5cm from beg.

**Armhole shaping**
**Next row** Ch 1, sl st in first dc, [sl st in next ch 1-sp and in next dc] 4 (4, 4, 5, 5) times, ch 5, 1 dc in next dc, cont in mesh pat to last 4 (4, 4, 5, 5) mesh sps and leave these sps unworked—4 (4, 4, 5, 5) mesh sps dec at each end of row, turn. Cont to dec 2 mesh sps at each end of next 1 (2, 2, 2, 2) rows, then dec 1 mesh sp at each end of next 2 (1, 2, 2, 3) rows—35 (36, 37, 38, 39) mesh sps. Work even until armhole measures 6½ (6½, 7, 7½, 8)"/16.5 (16.5, 17.5, 19, 20.5)cm.

**Neck and shoulder shaping**
**Next row** Work 10 (10, 10, 11, 11) mesh sps, leave center 15 (16, 17, 16, 17) sps unworked (for neck), rejoin 2nd skein MC to work last 10 (10, 10, 11, 11) mesh sps. Cont to work both sides at once with separate skeins of yarn, dec 5 sts from each neck edge once and, AT THE SAME TIME, when armhole measures 6½ (6½, 7, 7½, 8)"/17.5 (17.5, 19, 20.5, 21.5)cm, shape shoulders each side by dec 3 sts each side once, then 2 (2, 2, 3, 3) sts once.

## FRONT

Work as for back until armhole measures 2 (2, 2½, 3, 3½)"/5 (5, 6.5, 7.5, 9)cm.

**Neck opening**
**Next row** Work 17 (17, 18, 18, 19) mesh sps, leave center 1 (2, 1, 2, 1) mesh sps unworked, join 2nd skein MC and work to end. Cont to work both sides separately for 2"/5cm more.

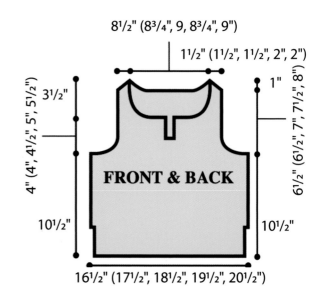

8½" (8¾", 9, 8¾", 9")
1½" (1½", 1½", 2", 2")
1"
3½"
4" (4", 4½", 5", 5½")
6½" (6½", 7", 7½", 8")
**FRONT & BACK**
10½"
10½"
16½" (17½", 18½", 19½", 20½")

Paul Amato

## Neck shaping

**Next row—First side** Work 11 (11, 12, 12, 13) mesh sps, leave rem 6 sps unworked.

**Second side** Leave first 6 sps unworked, rejoin MC and work rem 11 (11, 12, 12, 13) mesh sps. Cont to dec at neck edge every row in this way, dec 3 sts once, 2 sts once and 1 st 1 (1, 2, 1, 2) times—5 (5, 5, 6, 6) mesh sps. When same number of rows as back, shape shoulders as on back.

## FINISHING

Block pieces. Sew shoulder seams. Sew side seams (or sl st tog) taking in 1 mesh sp for a selvage at each seam.

## Edging

Working around armhole with MC and smaller hook, work 1 rnd sc evenly around armhole edge, pulling CC through last 2 lps on hook at end of rnd. Cut MC.

**Rnd 2** With CC, ch 3, work 1 dc in each sc around. Join with sl st to t-ch, fasten off, leaving a long end for sewing. Fold edge in half to WS and with tapestry needle, sew front lp of each dc to corresponding sc lp in MC along edge, forming corded edge. Work edge in same way around other armhole, lower and neck edges.

# LACY medallion tote

Francis Milon

# You'll Need

## YARN
- 5¼oz/150g, 330yd/ 300m of any DK weight cotton blend in white

## HOOKS
- One each sizes G/6 and H/8 (4mm and 5mm) crochet hooks *or size to obtain gauge*

## OTHER MATERIALS
- 2 wood beads

## FINISHED MEASUREMENTS
9"/23cm square

## GAUGE
1 square to 3"/7.5cm using smaller hook.
*Take time to check gauge.*

## BAG (make 2 pieces)
**Note** Squares are joined as they are worked. Work as indicated on diagram foll squares 1-9 for back, then rep for front.

### First square (A)
**With smaller hook, ch 8, join with sl st to form ring. **Rnd 1** Ch 3, 19 dc into ring, join with sl st to 3rd ch of beg ch. **Rnd 2** Ch 4, [dc 1 into next dc, ch 1] 19 times, end rnd with sl st into 3rd ch.** **Rnd 3** Sl st into next ch-1 space, ch 10, skip next ch-1 space (1 dc, 1 ch and 1 dc from previous rnd), *[2 dc into next ch-1 space] 4 times, ch 7 (corner), skip next ch-1 space, rep from * twice more; [2 dc into next ch-1 space] 3 times, 1 dc into next ch-1 space, sl st in 3rd ch. Fasten off.

### Join one side square (B)
Work as for first square from ** to **. **Rnd 3** Sl st into next ch-1 space, ch 10, skip next ch-1 space (1 dc, 1 ch and 1 dc from previous rnd), [2 dc into next ch-1 space] 4 times, ch 3, holding square to the right (or above) of square being joined, sl st into 4th ch of square being joined, ch 3, skip next ch-1 space, [2 dc into next ch-1 space] 2 times; join by sl st into space between 4th and 5th dc of square being joined; [2 dc into next ch-1 space] 2 times; ch 3, sl st into 4th ch of square being joined, ch 3, skip next ch-1 space, [2 dc into next ch-1 space] 4

times, ch 7, [2 dc into next ch-1 space] 3 times, 1 dc into next ch-1 space, sl st in 3rd ch. Fasten off.

### Join 2 sides square (C)
Work as for first square from ** to **. **Rnd 3** Sl st into next ch-1 space, ch 10, skip next ch-1 space (1 dc, 1 ch and 1 dc from previous rnd), [2 dc into next ch-1 space] 4 times, *ch 3, holding square to the right (or above) of square being joined, sl st into 4th ch of square being joined, ch 3, skip next ch-1 space, [2 dc into next ch-1 space] 2 times; join by sl st into space between 4th and 5th dc of square being joined; [2 dc into next ch-1 space] 2 times*; rep from * once more; ch 3, sl st into 4th ch of square being joined, ch 3, skip next ch-1 space, [2 dc into next ch-1 space] 3 times, 1 dc into next ch-1 space, sl st in 3rd ch. Fasten off.

## FINISHING
With WS tog, 2 strands of yarn and larger hook, join sides and bottom edge by working 1 row reverse sc. Fasten off. With RS of bag facing, 2 strands of yarn and larger hook, work 1 rnd reverse sc around upper edge, beg at side seam. Fasten off.

## STRAPS
With smaller hook and 1 strand of yarn, join yarn with sl st to top edge of bag at side seam, ch 75, join with 1 sc at opposite side seam. Make 3 more straps, always join with sc at side seams. Fasten off.

### Slide for straps
With smaller hook and 1 strand of yarn, ch 12, turn, 1 dc in 4th ch from hook, work 1 dc into each ch to end. Fasten off, leaving longer tail for seam. Wrap slide around all straps, sew seam.

### Drawstring
With smaller hook and 1 strand of yarn, ch 175. Fasten off. Thread in and out at top edge, beg at center front. Slip 1 bead onto each end, secure with knot.

PLACEMENT DIAGRAM

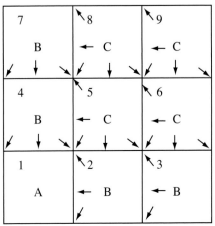

# NIGHT light

## FINISHED MEASUREMENTS
18 x 39"/45.5 x 99cm

## GAUGE
One medallion to 9"/23cm using size J/10 (6mm) crochet hook.
*Take time to check gauge.*

## MEDALLION A
Ch 8. Join ch with a sl st forming a ring. **Rnd 1** Ch 3 (counts as 1 dc), work 23 dc in ring. Join rnd with a sl st in 3rd ch of ch-3. **Rnd 2** Ch 5 (counts as 1 dc and ch 2), sk first st, *dc in next st, ch 2, sk next st; rep from * around 11 times. Join rnd with a sl st in 3rd ch of ch-5—12 ch-2 sps. **Rnd 3** Ch 4 (counts as 1 tr), work 3 tr in first ch-2 sp, *work 4 tr in next ch-2 sp; rep from * around 11 times. Join rnd with a sl st in 4th ch of ch-4. **Rnd 4** Ch 3 (counts as 1 dc), [yo, draw up a lp in next st, yo and draw through 2 lps on hook] 3 times, yo and draw through all 4 lps on hook, ch 6, *dc in next st, [yo, draw up a lp in next st, yo and draw through 2 lps on hook] 3 times, yo and draw through all 4 lps on hook, ch 6; rep from * around 11 times. Join rnd with a sl st in 3rd ch of ch-3—12 ch-6 lps. **Rnd 5** Ch 1 (counts as 1 sc), work 3 sc in first ch-6 lp, ch 3, sl st in last sc made (picot made), work 4 sc in same ch-6 lp, *work 4 sc in next ch-6 lp, ch 3, sl st in last sc made, work 4 sc in same ch-6 lp; rep from * around 11 times. Join rnd with a sl st in first ch of ch-1. Fasten off.

## MEDALLION B (make 14)
Work as for medallion A to rnd 5. **Rnd 5** (joining) Ch 1 (counts as 1 sc), work 3 sc in first ch-6 lp, ch 3, sl st in last sc made (picot made), work 4 sc in same ch-6 lp, * work 4 sc in next ch-6 lp, ch 3, sl st in last sc made, work 4 sc in same ch-6 lp; rep from * around 9 times, end [work 4 sc in next ch-6 lp, ch 1, sc in picot of medallion A (joining st), ch 1, work 4 sc in same ch-6 lp] twice.

Marco Zambelli

Join rnd with a sl st in first ch of ch-1. Fasten off.
Referring to medallion placement diagram, join next medallion B (on rnd 5) to medallion A and to first medallion B, working picot sts and joining sts wherever needed. Cont to join 12 rem medallions together following diagram.

## FINISHING
Lightly block piece to measurements.

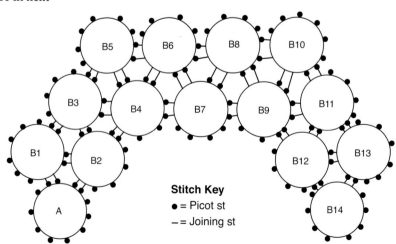

**Stitch Key**
- ● = Picot st
- — = Joining st

# UNDER wraps

## You'll Need

**YARN**

- 12¼oz/350g, 1200yd/1100m of any worsted weight wool blend in white

**HOOKS**

- Size G/6 (4.5mm) crochet hook *or size to obtain gauge*

## FINISHED MEASUREMENTS

Approx 63 x 35"/160 x 89cm

## GAUGE

Each shell pat measures 1¼"/3cm wide.
*Take time to check gauge.*

## STITCH GLOSSARY

**Shell pattern** (Dc, ch 1, dc, ch 1, dc, ch 1, dc, ch 1, dc) into next st.

## SHAWL

Ch 442.

**Row 1 (RS)** Sc into 2nd ch from hook, *skip next 4 ch, shell pat into next ch, skip next 4 ch, sc into next ch; rep from * to end. Ch 3, turn.

**Row 2** Skip sc and first dc, sc into next ch-1 sp, ch 2, skip next dc, sc into next dc, *ch 2, skip next dc, dc into next ch-1 sp, ch 2, skip next (dc, sc, and dc), dc into next ch-1 sp, ch 2, skip next dc, sc into next dc; rep from * leaving last 2 dc and sc unworked. Ch 1, turn.

**Row 3** Skip first sc and next dc, *shell into next ch-2 sp, sc into next sc, skip next ch-2 sp and next dc; rep from *, leaving last ch-2 sp and ch-3 t-ch unworked. Ch 3, turn.

Rep rows 2 and 3 until only one shell rem, ending with a row 3.

**Next row** Skip next dc, sc into next ch-1 sp, ch 3, skip next dc, sc into next dc, ch 3, skip next dc, sc into next ch-1 sp, *ch 3, skip next dc, sc into next dc, ch 3, skip next dc, sc into next ch-1 sp; rep from * along side, ending with ch 3, sk next dc, sc into last sc. Ch 6, turn.

**Next row** *Sc into next ch-sp, ch 4; rep from * around all 3 sides, ending with sc into next ch-sp, ch 3, dc into last st.

Fasten off.

Paul Amato

## You'll Need

**YARN**

- *Baby Sheen* by Red Heart, 3½oz/100g, 307yd/281m acrylic
- 4 (5) balls #001 white

**HOOK**

- Size D/3 (3mm) crochet hook *or size to obtain gauge*

**OTHER MATERIALS**

- Five ½"/13mm buttons

## SIZES

Sized for Small/Medium (Large/X-Large). Shown in size Small/Medium.

## FINISHED MEASUREMENTS

**Bust (buttoned)** 35 (44)"/89 (112) cm
**Length** 18½ (20)"/47 (51)cm
**Upper arm** 16½ (18)"/42 (46)cm

## GAUGE

2 lace pat reps to 4½"/11.5cm and 21 rows to 8"/20.5cm in lace pat using size D/3 (3mm) hook.
*Take time to check gauge.*

## STITCH GLOSSARY

**Lace pattern stitch**
Chain a multiple of 12 plus 6.
**Row 1 (RS)** (Dc, ch 2, dc) in 5th ch from hook, ch 4, skip next 5 ch, *(dc, ch 2, dc) in next ch for v-st, ch 4, skip next 5 ch; rep from * to last 2 ch, v-st in next ch, dc in last ch, turn. **Row 2** Ch 3, *work v-st in ch-2 sp of next v-st, ch 3, (3 dc, ch 2, 3 dc) in ch-2 sp of next v-st for shell, ch 3; rep from * to last v-st, v-st in ch-2 sp of last v-st, dc in top of t-ch, turn. **Row 3** Ch 3, *v-st in ch-2 sp of next v-st, ch

4, v-st in ch-2 sp of next shell, ch 4; rep from * to last v-st, v-st in ch-2 sp of last v-st, dc in top of t-ch, turn. Rep rows 2 and 3 for lace pat st.

## BACK

Ch 102 (126). Work in lace pat on 8 (10) lace pat reps for 25 (27) rows. Cut yarn. Turn work.
**Armhole shaping**
With WS of work facing, rejoin yarn in first dc of 3rd v-st from beg of row, ch 3, [work v-st in next v-st, ch 3, work shell in next v-st, ch 3] 6 (8) times, work v-st in next v-st, dc in next ch, turn. Cont in lace pat st on these 6 (8) lace pats for 21 (23) rows more. Fasten off.

## LEFT FRONT

Ch 54 (66). Work in lace pat on 4 (5) lace pat reps for 25 (27) rows.
**Armhole and neck shaping**
**Row 1 (WS)** Pat to last 3 v-sts, v-st in next v-st, dc in next ch, turn. **Row 2** Pat to last v-st, dc in last v-st, turn. **Row 3** Ch 6, work shell in next v-st, pat to end, turn. **Row 4** Pat to last shell, v-st in last shell, ch 2, dc in 3rd ch of t-ch, turn. **Row 5** Ch 3, work shell in next v-st, pat to end, turn. **Row 6** Pat to last shell, v-st in last shell, skip 2 dc, dc in next dc, turn. **Row 7** Ch 3, 3 dc in first v-st, pat to end, turn. **Row 8** Pat to last v-st, v-st in last v-st, ch 4, dc in top of t-ch, turn. **Row 9** Ch 6, v-st in next v-st, pat to end, turn. **Row 10** Pat to last v-st, v-st in last v-st, ch 2, dc in 3rd ch of t-ch, turn. **Row 11** Ch 3, v-st in first v-st, pat to end, turn. **Rows 12-15** Rep rows 2-5. **Row 16** Pat to last shell, v-st in last shell, ch 1, dc in top of t-ch, turn. **Row 17** Ch 3, work shell in first v-st, pat to end, turn. Rep last 2 rows 2 (3) times more, then rep row 16 again. Fasten off.

## RIGHT FRONT

Work as for left front (lace pat is reversible).

## SLEEVES

Ch 54 (66). Work in lace pat on 4 (5) lace pats for 2 rows.
**Sleeve shaping**
**Row 1** Ch 5, v-st in first v-st, pat to last v-st, v-st in last v-st, ch 2, dc in top of t-ch, turn. **Row 2** Ch 5, v-st in next v-st, pat to last v-st, v-st in last v-st, ch 2, dc in 3rd ch of t-ch, turn. **Rows 3 and 4** Rep row 2. **Row 5** Ch 7, v-st in next v-st, pat to last v-st, v-st in last v-st, ch 4, dc in 3rd ch of t-ch, turn. **Row 6** Ch 3, 2 dc in first dc, ch 3, v-st in next v-st pat to last v-st, v-st in last v-st, ch 3, 3 dc in 5th ch of t-ch, turn. **Row 7** Ch 5, dc in first dc, ch 4, v-st in next v-st, pat to last v-st, v-st in last v-st, ch 4, (dc, ch 2, dc) in top of t-ch, turn.
**Row 8** Ch 5, 3 dc in first ch-2 sp, ch 3, v-st in next v-st, pat to last complete v-st, v-st in this v-st, ch 3, 3 dc in t-ch

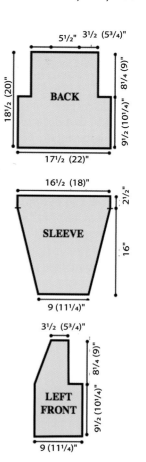

Marco Zambelli

v-st in first ch-2 sp, pat to t-ch sp, v-st in t-ch sp, dc in 3rd ch of t-ch, turn. **Row 24** Ch 3, v-st in first v-st, pat to last v-st, v-st in last v-st, dc in top of t-ch, turn. Rep rows 1 to 14 (10) again, then work 5 (9) rows even as established in lace pat. Place a yarn marker at each end of last row, then work 6 rows even in lace pat as established. Fasten off.

## FINISHING
Block pieces very lightly.
**Back lower border**
With RS facing, rejoin yarn in base of first ch at lower edge of back, ch 1, then work 1 sc in base of each ch to end—99 (123) sc.
**Row 1** Ch 3, v-st in 2nd sc, *skip 2 sc, v-st in next sc; rep from * to last sc, dc in last sc, turn. **Row 2** *Ch 3, sc in sp between next 2 v-sts; rep from * ending ch 3, sc in top of t-ch, turn. **Row 3** Ch 1, *4 sc in next ch-3 sp; rep from * ending sl st in first ch of row 2. Fasten off.
**Front lower borders**
With RS facing, rejoin yarn in base of first ch at lower edge of each front, ch 1, then work 1 sc in base of each ch to end—51 (63) sc. Complete as for back lower borders.
**Sleeve lower borders**
With RS facing, rejoin yarn in base of first ch at lower edge of sleeve, ch 1, then work 1 sc in base of each ch to end—51 (63) sc. Complete as for back lower border.
**Front and neck border**
With RS facing, rejoin yarn at lower inner edge of right front border, ch 1 and sc evenly up right front, across back neck and down left front, working a multiple of 3 sc. Complete as for back lower border. Using ch-2 sp of v-st on border for buttonholes, mark position of 5 buttonholes on right front border, with the first one in 2nd v-st, the last one at 1"/2.5cm below neck shaping and the others spaced evenly between. Sew on buttons opposite buttonholes.

sp, ch 2, dc in 3rd ch of t-ch, turn. **Row 9** Ch 5, dc in first ch-2 sp, ch 4, v-st in next v-st, pat to last v-st, v-st in last v-st, ch 4, dc in t-ch sp, ch 2, dc in 3rd ch of t-ch, turn.
**Row 10** Rep row 8. **Row 11** Ch 3, v-st in first ch-2 sp, pat to last v-st, v-st in last v-st, ch 4, v-st in t-ch sp, dc in 3rd ch of t-ch, turn. **Row 12** Ch 3, (2 dc, ch 2, 3 dc) in first v-st, ch 3, pat to last v-st, (3 dc, ch 2, 2 dc) in last v-st, dc in top of t-ch, turn. **Row 13** Ch 5, v-st in first shell, pat to last shell, v-st in last shell, ch 2, dc in top of t-ch, turn. **Row 14** Ch 4, work shell in first v-st, pat to last v-st, work shell in last v-st, ch 1, dc in 3rd ch of t-ch, turn. **Rows 15 and 16** Rep rows 13 and 14. **Row 17** Ch 7, v-st in first shell, pat to last shell, v-st in last shell, ch 4, dc in 2nd ch of t-ch, turn. **Row 18** Ch 6, work shell in first v-st, pat to last v-st, work shell in last v-st, ch 3, dc in 5th ch of t-ch, turn. **Row 19** Ch 5, dc in first dc, ch 4, v-st in first shell, pat to last shell, v-st in last shell, ch 4, (dc, ch 2, dc) in 4th ch of t-ch, turn. **Row 20** Ch 5, dc in first ch-2 sp, ch 3, work shell in next v-st, pat to last complete v-st, work shell in this v-st, ch 3, dc in t-ch sp, ch 2, dc in 3rd ch of t-ch, turn. **Row 21** Ch 5, dc in first ch-2 sp, ch 4, v-st in next shell, pat to last shell, v-st in last shell, ch 4, dc in t-ch sp, ch 2, dc in 3rd ch of t-ch, turn. **Row 22** Rep row 20. **Row 23** Ch 3,

# SUMMER shoppers

## You'll Need

**Square Tote**

YARN ❹
- 10½oz/300g, 720yd/660m of any worsted weight acrylic in turquoise

HOOKS
- Size F/5 (4mm) crochet hook *or size to obtain gauge*

OTHER MATERIALS
- 1yd/1m of lining fabric
- 2yd of ½"/1.25cm horse-hair braid
- Large snap closure
- One 11¼ x 3¾"/28.5 x 9.5cm plastic or heavy cardboard for base insert

**Knapsack**

YARN ❹
- 14oz/400g, 960yd/880m of any worsted weight acrylic in lavender

HOOKS
- One each sizes B/1 and F/5 (2 and 4mm) crochet hooks *or size to obtain gauge*

OTHER MATERIALS
- 1yd/1m of lining fabric
- Large snap closure
- 2 small buttons

## FINISHED MEASUREMENTS

**Square Tote**
10" long x 12" wide/25.5cm x 30.5cm
**Gusset measures** 4"/10cm wide.

**Knapsack**
**Bottom diameter** 12"/30.5cm
**Depth** 12"/30.5cm

## GAUGE

**Square Tote**
18 dc to 4"/10cm and 17 dc rows to 8"/20cm over dc pat using larger hook.
*Take time to check gauge.*

**Knapsack**
18 dc to 4"/10cm and 10 dc rnds to 4½"/ 11.5cm using larger hook.
*Take time to check gauge.*

## SQUARE TOTE

**Gussets and bottom**
Ch 20. **Row 1** Dc in 4th ch from hook and in each ch to end—18 dc, counting t-ch as 1 dc. Ch 3, turn. **Row 2** Skip first dc, 1 dc in each dc, end 1 dc in top of t-ch. Ch 3, turn. Rep row 2 until there are 67 rows from beg. Fasten off.
**Front**
Place 4 markers on each side of row 22 and row 46 of gusset piece to mark center 25 rows of piece (this marks bottom of bag). Working across one side from marker to marker, work 51 sc evenly along one side of bottom. Ch 3, turn. Work even in 51 dc for 7 rows more. **Row 9** Ch 4, skip first 2 dc, *dc in next dc, ch 1, skip next dc; rep from *, end dc in top of t-ch—25 mesh sps. **Rows 10 and 11** Ch 4, *dc in next dc, ch 1; rep from *, end dc in top of t-ch. **Row 12** Ch 4, skip first dc mesh sp, dc in next dc, work dc mesh to last dc mesh sp, skip last dc mesh sp, turn. **Row 13** Rep row 12—21 mesh

sps. **Rows 14 and 15** Work even in mesh pat. **Row 16** Ch 3, work 1 dc in each dc and in each ch-1 sp to end—43 dc. Work even in dc for 6 rows more. Fasten off.
**Back**
Working along other side of bottom, between opposite markers, work as for front.

## FINISHING
Pin to measurements and steam lightly. Working from RS over horsehair braid, sc one gusset to side of front, cont to sc across gusset (at bottom edge), sc other gusset to side of back. Repeat for other side of bag. Secure ends. Working from left to right, work reverse sc edge around top of bag.

## HANDLES (make 2)
Cut 4 lengths of yarn to form into a twisted cord 21"/53cm long. Form one end into a 1½"/4cm tassel. Knot and fringe opposite end to make a tassel to match. Make a chain the length of the twisted cord. Hold chain underneath twisted cord and working over cord and through 1 ch at same time, work 1 sc around cord and through each ch. Fasten off. Secure handles to bag for 2"/5cm at top, at center 5½"/14cm of bag. Cut fabric to cover base insert with ½"/1.25cm seam allowance and hand-sew to fit. Cut fabric to match front and back pieces and gusset and bottom piece with a seam allowance of ½"/1.25cm. Seam gusset to front and back pieces. Press lining down 1"/2.5cm at top and tack to inside of bag. Sew snap inside to center for closing.

## KNAPSACK
**Bottom circle**
With larger hook, beg at center, ch 8, join with sl st to first ch to form ring.
**Rnd 1** Ch 2 (does not count as 1 dc)

Brian Kraus

work 19 dc into ring. Join with sl st to top of first dc. **Rnd 2** Ch 2 (does not count as 1 dc), [1 dc in next dc, 2 dc in next dc] 9 times, 1 dc in last dc—28 dc. Join with sl st to top of first dc. **Rnd 3** Ch 2, 1 dc in each of first 2 dc, [2 dc in next dc, 1 dc in next dc] 13 times—41 dc. Join with sl st. **Rnd 4** Ch 2, 1 dc in first dc, [2 dc in next dc, 1 dc in next dc] 20 times—61 dc. Join. **Rnd 5** Ch 2, 1 dc in first dc, 2 dc in next dc, 1 dc in next dc, [2 dc in next dc, 1 dc in each of next 4 dc] 11 times, 2 dc in next dc, 1 dc in each of last 2 dc—74 dc. Join. **Rnd 6** Ch 2, 1 dc in each of first 4 dc, [2 dc in next dc, 1 dc in each of next 4 dc] 14 times—88 dc. Join. **Rnd 7** Working in dc, inc 14 dc evenly around (having 1 more dc between incs) as before—102 dc. Join. **Rnd 8** Rep rnd 7—116 dc. **Rnd 9** Rep rnd 7—130 dc. **Rnd 10** Working in dc, inc 12 dc evenly around— 142 dc. **Rnds 11 and 12** Work even in 142 dc. **Rnd 13** Ch 4, *skip 1 dc (or st), 1 dc in next dc (or st), ch 1; rep from * end sl st in 3rd ch of ch 4. **Rnd 14** Ch 1, sc in each dc and ch-1 sp around. Rep last 2 rnds for mesh pat 16 times more. Then rep rnd 14 (sc every rnd) for 5 more rnds. Fasten off.

### Flap

With smaller hook, ch 26. **Row 1** Sc in 2nd ch from hook and in each ch to end—25 sc. Rep row 1 until piece measures

6½"/16.5cm from beg. Dec 1 sc each end of next 5 rows. Working around outside edge of flap, work 1 sc evenly around entire outside edge, working 3 sc in each corner. Fasten off.

## FINISHING

Pin pieces to measurements and steam lightly. Cut lining fabric to match bottom circle, the inside tube of bag and the flap, leaving ½"/1.25cm for seam allowances and 1"/2.5cm at top. Sew sides into tube, sew base circle into tube. Press under seam allowance at top. Tack to bag ½"/1.25cm below top. Sew lining to flap. Cut 4 lengths of yarn to make a 40"/102cm twisted cord. Make cord and thread through top of mesh sps.

### Cord stay

With smaller hook, ch 22, join with sl st to first ch to form ring. **Rnd 1** Work 1 sc in each ch around, ch 1 join. Rep rnd 1 four times more. Fasten off. Fold stay at center and tack through both thicknesses at center forming a figure 8. Place on ends of cord for holding in place.

## STRAPS (make 2)

With smaller hook, ch 130. Sc in 2nd ch from hook and in each ch to end. Do not turn, but working into other side (beg lps) of ch, work 1 sc in each lp to end, 2 sc in last lp. Then work 1 sc in each sc all around both sides (with 2 sc in other corner). Fasten off. Centering straps 2½"/6.5cm apart at upper center back and beg at 1 mesh row below top, sew one strap securely for about 1"/2.5cm. Centering straps at 8"/20cm apart at lower center back and sewing into 2nd dc row at bottom, sew straps securely at bottom. Sew one button to center of each bottom strap beg at 3"/7.5cm down from center back, sew straight edge of flap over straps. Sew one half of snap to center of flap, one half of snap to corresponding center front of bag.

# TOTE-A-TOTE

## You'll Need

### Tote

**YARN** [4]
- 14oz/400g, 920yd/840m of any worsted weight acrylic in turquoise

**HOOKS**
- Size E/4 (3.5mm) crochet hook *or size to obtain gauge*

**OTHER MATERIALS**
- 1yd/1m of lining fabric
- Large snap closure

### Sack

**YARN** [4]
- 14oz/400g, 860yd/790m of any worsted weight acrylic in periwinkle

**HOOKS**
- Size E/4 (3.5mm) crochet hook *or size to obtain gauge*

**OTHER MATERIALS**
- One ⅞"/22mm button
- 1yd/1m flexible plastic ¼"/6mm tube
- 1yd/1m of lining fabric

## FINISHED MEASUREMENTS

**Patchwork Tote**
12½" long x 11" wide/32cm x 28cm

**Sack**
**Bottom piece** 7" long x 4" wide/18cm x10cm
11" tall x 15"wide at top/28cm x 38cm

## STITCH GLOSSARY

**Woven Pattern Stitch**
**Rnd 1** Ch 1, sc in first st, *insert hook 1 row below next sc and work 1 sc in this sp (for 1 sc below), sc in next st; rep from *, end 1 sc below.
**Rnd 2** Ch 1, *1 sc below, 1 sc in next st; rep from * to end.
Rep rnds 1 and 2 for woven pat st

## GAUGES

**Patchwork Tote**
One square to 3½"/9cm square using size E/4 (3.5mm) hook.
**Sack**
15 sc and 21 rows to 4"/10cm over woven pat st using size E/4 (3.5mm) hook.
*Take time to check gauge.*

## PATCHWORK TOTE

**Square** (make 18)
Beg at center, ch 8, join with sl st to first ch to form ring. **Rnd 1** Working into ring, *work 1 sc into ring, ch 3; rep from * 7 times more, end sl st into top of sc—8 lps. **Rnd 2** Ch 4, holding lp from previous rnd forward and working into beg ring from behind, *work 1 sc in ring, ch 4; rep from * 6 times more, end sl st into ring—8 lps. **Rnd 3** In each ch-4 lp, work 1 sc, ch 1, 2 dc, ch 1, 1 sl st—8 petals. Join with sl st to first sc. **Rnd 4** *Ch 4, holding petal from previous rnd forward, work 1 sc around sc post from behind; rep from * 7 times more—8 lps. Join with sl st to first lp. **Rnd 5** Rep rnd 3. **Rnd 6** *Work 1 sc in first ch-1 sp of petal, ch 8, skip 2 dc, 1 sc in next ch-1 sp of same petal (corner), ch 4, 1 sc in between 2 dc of next petal, ch 4; rep from * 3 times more, join with sl st to first sc. **Rnd 7** *Work 4 sc, ch 1, 4 sc in ch-8 lp, [4 sc in ch-4 lp] twice; rep from *, join with sl st to first sc. **Rnd 8** Ch 1, work 1 sc in each sc and 3 sc in each ch-1 corner sp around. Fasten off.

## FINISHING

Pin squares to measurements and steam lightly. Sew squares tog with 3 sets and rows of squares each for back and front. Sew front and back tog along 3 sides.
**Top edge**
Sc evenly around top edge of bag. Join with sl st, ch 1. Work 7 more rnds sc. Fasten off.

## STRAPS

(make 2)
Ch 100. Sc in 2nd ch from hook and each ch to end. Do not turn, but working into other side (beg lps) of ch, work 1 sc in each lp to end, 2 sc in last lp. Then work 1 sc in each sc all around both sides (with 2 sc in other corner). Fasten off. Overlap each strap by 3"/7.5cm from top of bag centering each side of center square. Sew to bag. Cut lining fabric 24"/61cm long by 23"/59cm wide. Fold in half lengthwise and with ½"/1.25cm seams, sew along one long side and lower edge. Press 1"/2.5cm at top to WS. Hand-sew lining to inside of bag ½"/1.25cm down from top. Sew snap inside at center for closing.

## SACK

**Bottom Piece**
Ch 15. **Rnd 1** Work 2 sc in 2nd ch from hook, sc in each of next 12 ch, 2 sc in last ch, do not turn, but turn ch upside down and working along opposite side (beg ch lps), work 2 sc in first lp, 1 sc in each of next 12 lps, 2 sc in last

lp—32 sts. Join with sl st to first sc. **Rnd 2** Ch 1, work 2 sc in each of first 2 sts, sc in next 13 sts, 2 sc in each of next 3 sts, sc in next 13 sts, 2 sc in last st—38 sts. **Rnds 3-8** Rep rnd 2, adding 3 sts at each end of piece (6 sts total each rnd) and having 3 more sts between incs each side every rnd —74 sts. End of bottom piece. Cut piece of plastic tubing 17½"/45cm long to fit outside edge of bottom piece. **Rnd 9** Laying plastic tubing around outside, work 1 sc over tubing and through each sc around, join.

### Beg Main Bag

**Rnds 10 and 11** Work even in sc. **Rnd 12** Ch 1, [sc in each of next 4 sts, 2 sc in next st (inc), sc in each of next 3 sts, inc 1 in next sc] 8 times, sc in each of last 2 sts—90 sts. **Rnd 13** Ch 1, sc in first st, *insert hook 1 row below next sc and work 1 sc in this sp (for 1 sc below), sc in next st; rep from *, end 1 sc below. **Rnd 14** Ch 1, *1 sc below, 1 sc in next st; rep from * to end. Rep rnds 13 and 14 for woven pat st for 8 more rnds. **Rnd 23** Ch 1, *work 3 sts in next st, work next 17 sts in pat; rep from * 4 times more—100 sts. **Rnds 24-33** Work even in pat. **Rnd 34** Ch 1, *work 19 sts, work 3 sts in next st; rep from * 4 times more—110 sts. Work even in woven pat st until bag measures 9½"/24cm from bottom piece. Work even in sc only for 5 rnds. Fasten off.

## FINISHING

Block pieces lightly. Cut lining to fit shaped base, allowing ½"/1.5cm seam allowance all around. Cut lining 13"/33cm long and 32"/81cm wide for inside of bag. Sew short sides tog to form tube. Gather one side to fit base piece. Sew sides to base.

### Chain Loop

Ch 32. Sc in 2nd ch and in each ch to end. Fold loop in half and sew securely at center back.

## STRAPS (make 2)

Ch 100. Sc in 2nd ch from hook and in each ch to end. Do not turn, but working into other side (beg lps) of ch, work 1 sc in each lp to end, 2 sc in last lp. Then work 1 sc in each sc all around both sides (with 2 sc in other corner). Fasten off. Centering straps at 4"/10cm on front and back, sew securely to bag for 1"/2.5cm each end. Sew on button opposite loop. Turn under top section of lining 1"/2.5cm and hand-sew to inside of bag.

Brian Kraus

# WRAP star

Nick Norwood

![] (difficulty rating: 3 of 4 filled)

## FINISHED MEASUREMENTS

66"/167.5cm wide by 38"/96.5cm long

## GAUGE

30 sts and 13 rows to 4"/10cm over pat st using size E/4 (3.5mm) crochet hook.

*Take time to check gauge.*

## STITCH GLOSSARY

**TC (triple cross)**
Sk next 2 sts. Dc in 3rd st, dc in 2nd st sk, dc in first st sk.

## SHAWL

Beg at bottom point, ch 8.
**Row 1 (WS)** Work 2 dc in 4th ch from

## You'll Need

### YARN 🧶 1
- 8oz/250g, 2500yd/ 2300m of any fingering weight wool blend in pink

### HOOK
- Size E/4 (3.5mm) crochet hook *or size to obtain gauge*

hook, dc in next 3 ch, work 2 dc in last ch—7 sts. Ch 3, turn. **Row 2** Work 3 dc in first st, dc in next st, TC over next 3 sts, dc in next st, work 3 dc in last st—11 sts. Ch 3, turn. **Row 3** Work 3 dc in first st, *TC over next 3 sts; rep from *, end work 3 dc in last st—15 sts. Ch 3, turn. **Row 4** Work 3 dc in first st, dc in next 2 sts, *TC over next 3 sts; rep from *, end dc in next 2 sts, work 3 dc in last st—19 sts. Ch 3, turn. **Row 5** Work 3 dc in first st, dc in next st, *TC over next 3 sts; rep from *, end dc in next st, work 3 dc in last st—23 sts. Ch 3, turn. **Row 6** Work 3 dc in first st, *TC over next 3 sts; rep from *, end work 3 dc in last st—27 sts. Ch 3, turn. Rep rows 4-6 for 35 times more—111 rows completed (piece should measure approx 35½/89cm from beg).

## EDGING

Ch 1, turn. **Rnd 1 (RS)** Sc in each dc across last row made, then making sure that work lies flat, sc evenly across each side edge. Join rnd with a sl st in ch-1. Ch 5, turn. Work back and forth across side edges only.

## RUFFLE

**Row 1 (WS)** Sk first st, sc in next st, *ch 5, sk next st, sc in next st; rep from * to end. Ch 5, turn. **Rows 2-9** *Sc in next ch-5 lp, ch 5; rep from *, end sc in last st. Ch 5, turn. After row 9 is completed, ch 1, turn. **Row 10 (RS)** Work 5 sc in each ch-5 lp across. Fasten off.

## FINISHING

Block piece to measurements.

Nick Norwood

# NATURAL
# beauty

## You'll Need

YARN ②
· 1¾oz/50g, 136yd/125m of any sport weight cotton blend in white

HOOKS
· One each sizes E/4 (3.5mm) and G/6 (4.5mm) crochet *or size to obtain gauge*

## FINISHED MEASUREMENTS
· **Head circumference** 20"/51cm
· **Depth** 6½"/16.5cm

## GAUGE
3 cluster pats and 4 rnds to 4"/10cm using size G/6 (4.5mm) hook.
*Take time to check gauge.*

## CAP
Beg at crown, with size G/6 hook, ch 4, join with sl st to first ch to form ring.
**Rnd 1** Work 9 sc into ring, join with sl st to first sc.
**Rnd 2** Ch 1, work 2 sc in each sc around, join with sl st to first sc—18 sc.
**Rnd 3** Ch 3, * in next sc work 1 dc, ch 2 and 1 dc (for V-st), skip 2 sc, ch 3; rep from * 5 times more, end by joining with sl st in top of first ch-3—6 V-sts.
**Rnd 4** Ch 4, *5tr in ch 2-sp (for cluster), skip ch-3 sp, ch 2; rep from * 5 times more, end with sl st in top of ch-4—6 clusters.
**Rnd 5** Ch 6, *skip 2 tr, in next tr work 1 dc, ch 2 and 1 dc (for V-st), ch 3, in next ch-2 sp work V-st, ch 3; rep from * end skip 2tr, in next tr work V-st, ch 3, dc in same sp with ch-6, ch 2, sl st in 3rd ch of ch-6—12 V-sts.
**Rnd 6** Ch 6, *5 tr in next V-st, ch 3; rep from * 11 times more, end join with sl st in 4th ch of ch-6—12 clusters.

**Rnd 7** Ch 6, *[in center tr of next 5-tr cluster work 1 V-st, ch 3] 3 times, V-st in next ch-3 sp, ch 3; rep from * twice more, then [in center tr of next 5-tr cluster work V-st, ch 3] 3 times, sl st in 3rd ch of ch-6—15 V-sts.
**Rnd 8** Ch 6, *5 tr in next V-st, ch 2; rep from * 14 times more, end join with sl st in 4th ch of ch 6—15 clusters.
**Rnd 9** Ch 6, * in center of next 5-tr cluster work 1 V-st, ch 3; rep from * 14 times more, end with sl st in 3rd ch of ch-6—15 V-sts.
**Rnds 10 and 12** Rep rnd 8.
**Rnd 11** Rep rnd 9.
**Rnd 13** Ch 1, * work 1 sc in ch-2 sp, 1 sc in each of 5 tr; rep from *, end 1 sc in last ch-2 sp, join with sl to first sc—91 sc.
**Rnd 14** Ch 3, skip next sc, *1 dc in next 2 sc, ch 1, skip 1 sc; rep from *, end sl st to 2nd ch of ch-3. Change to size E/4 (3.5mm) hook and turn to WS to work last 2 rnds from WS.
**Rnd 15 (WS)** Ch 1, work 1 sc in each dc and in each ch-1 around.
**Rnd 16 (WS)** Ch 3, skip first sc, * work 1 dc and 1 hdc in next sc, sl st in next sc; rep from * around. Fasten off.

# TAKE it easy

Dan Howell

## You'll Need

### YARN

- 29¾oz/850g, 1500yd/ 1275m of any worsted weight wool blend in tan

### HOOKS

- Size K/10½ (6.5mm) crochet hook *or size to obtain gauge*

## FINISHED MEASUREMENTS

Approx 33 x 55"/84 x 140cm

## GAUGE

5 mesh (ch 3, sc) to 5½"/14cm and 10 rows to 4"/10cm over pat st using size K/10½ (6.5mm) crochet hook. *Take time to check gauge.*

## STITCH GLOSSARY

**Pattern stitch**

(multiple of 3 sts)

**Row 1** Work 1 sc in 3rd ch from hook *ch 3, sk 2 sc, sc in next ch; rep from *, end with a sc in last ch.

**Row 2** *Ch 3, sc in next ch-3 sp; rep from *, end sc in last ch-3.

Rep row 2 for pat st.

## SHAWL

Ch 144. Work in pat st until piece measures 55"/140cm. Fasten off.

## FINISHING

With RS facing, work 1 rnd sc evenly around outside edge of shawl. Fasten off.